Mel Bay Presents

INSTANT RECITAL
LEVEL TWO

by Uri Ayn Rovner

- New Recital/Contest Selections
- Variety of Composers
- "Authentic" Form
- Carefully Chosen for Grade Level
- All Selections "Performance Oriented"

Visit us on the Web at www.melbay.com — E-mail us at email@melbay.com

FOREWORD

In the "Instant Recital" Series, students have a variety of shorter works that have been carefully chosen or written for performance in recitals or contests. They are fun to play and fun to hear. The selections are in authentic form so that each may be used for audition or to demonstrate achievement.

Each volume spans hundreds of years of piano composition by those composers who taught piano and wrote specifically for their students.

Use the "Instant Recital" Series as a supplement to any method book or music program, and open the doors to happy performing!

TO THE TEACHER

The selections for recital in this volume offer a variety of styles for the advanced beginner through intermediate piano student. Most of these compositions are rarely heard. They have been included here to introduce new "historical" material in authentic form.

Composers and their music are arranged chronologically, except for the Stephen Heller selection which was placed last to avoid inconvenient page turns. The teacher should assign pieces to be played in an order that can motivate and bring out the individual student's talents. Musical markings such as dynamics and fingerings, in some cases, have been added to assist in preparation and performance.

CONTENTS

1. Georg Philipp Telemann
   Vite in D (from 3rd Fantasie).................................... 7
   Vite in B♭ (from 5th Fantasie) 8

2. Robert Bremner
   Tamo Tanto 9

3. Benjamin Carr
   Duke of Kent's Grand March....................................... 10

4. Ludwig van Beethoven
   Zwei Deutsche 11

5. Franz Peter Schubert
   Ländler 13

6. Jean Baptiste Duvernoy
   Etude in F... 14

7. Johann Friedrich Burgmüller
   Consolation 16

8. Jean Louis Gobbaerts
   Melodie 18

9. Uri Ayn Rovner
   Monodique.. 20
   Parade... 22

10. Stephen Heller
    Song Without Words 24

VITE IN D

VITE IN B♭

ROBERT BREMNER (?1713–1789)
A publisher as well as a composer, Bremner's specialty was the music of his native land, Scotland. This selection comes from *The Harpsichord or Spinnet Miscellany,* which is a lesson book he wrote for beginning performers. Though authentic, ornaments may be considered optional.

TAMO TANTO

Robert Bremner

DUKE OF KENT'S GRAND MARCH

Majestically

Benjamin Carr

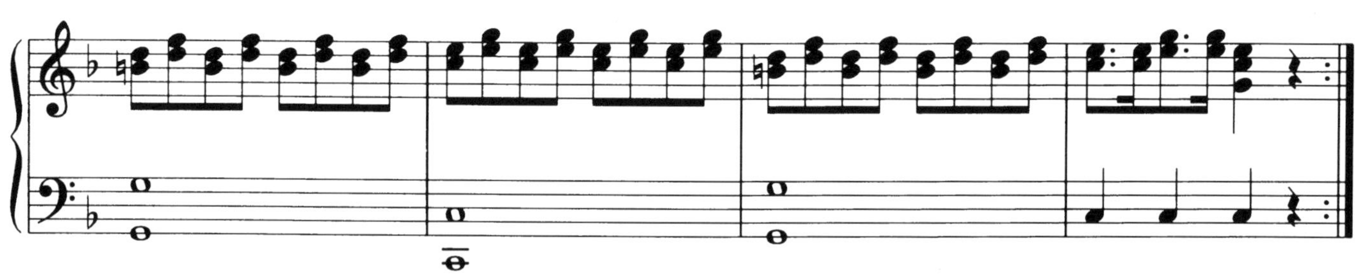

ZWEI DEUTSCHE

I

Ludwig van Beethoven

II

Moderato

Ludwig van Beethoven

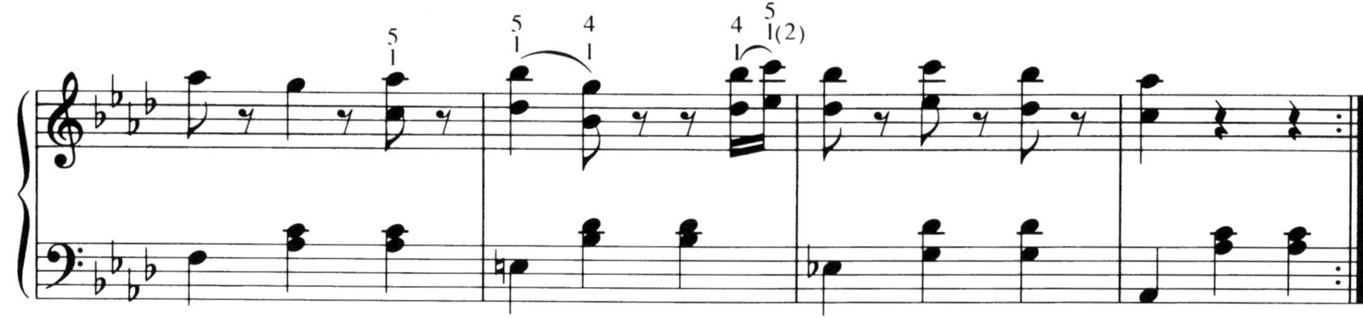

D.C. Deutsche I (No repeats)

LÄNDLER

Franz Schubert

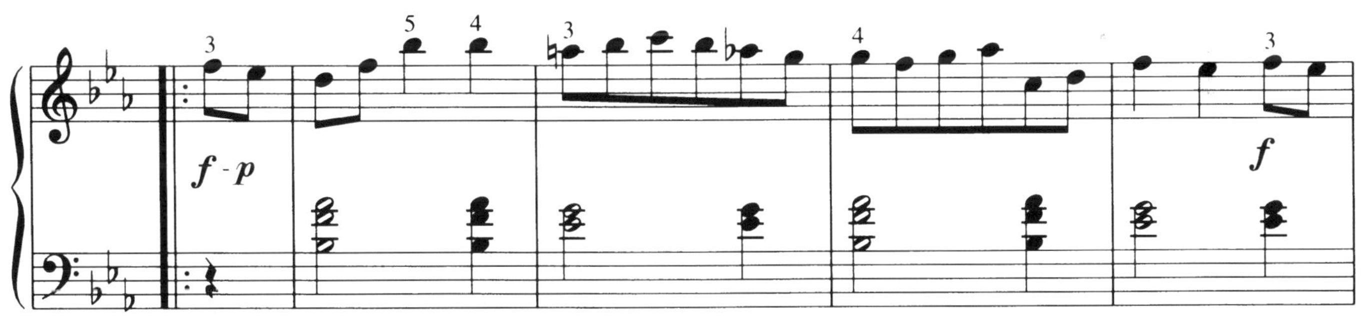

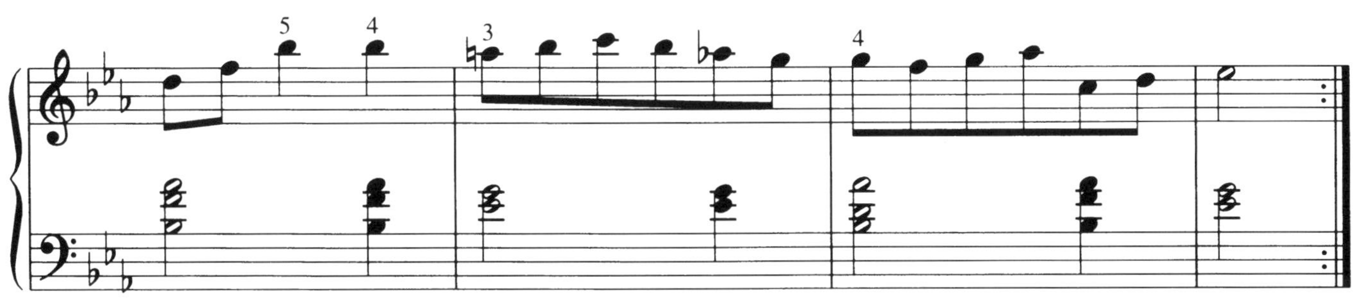

ETUDE IN F

Jean Baptiste Duvernoy

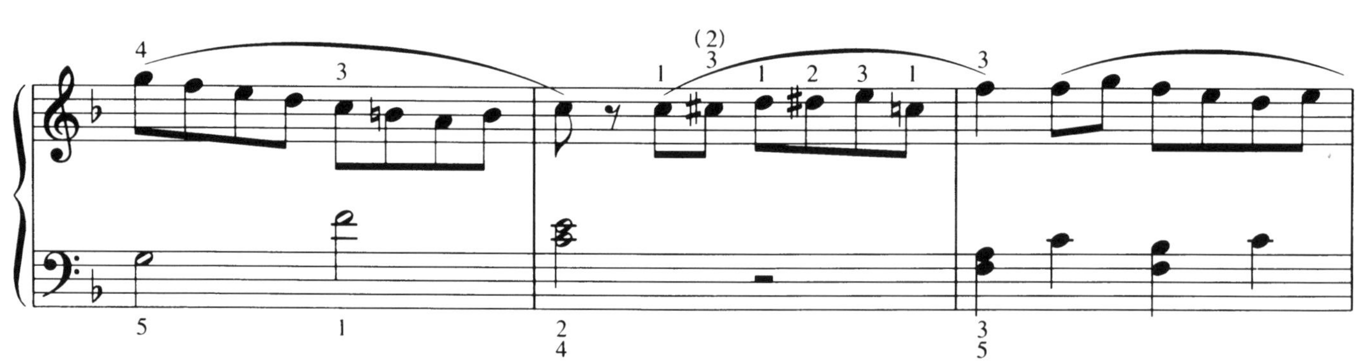

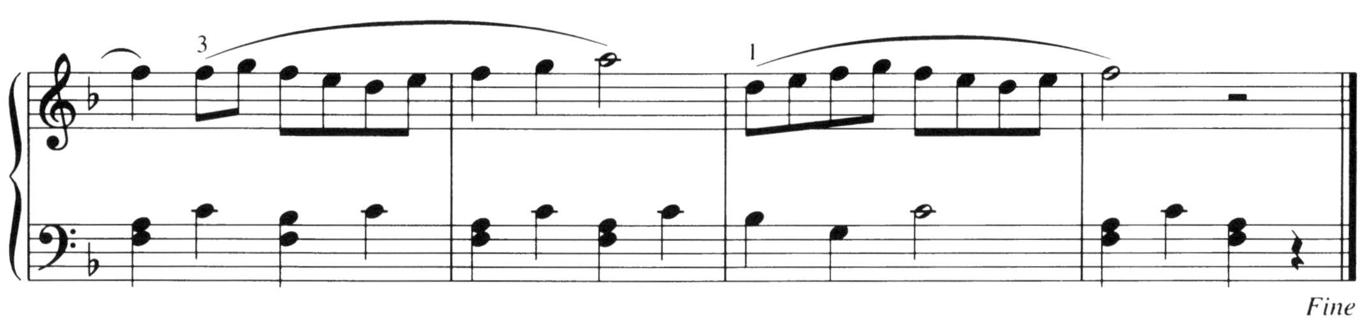

Fine

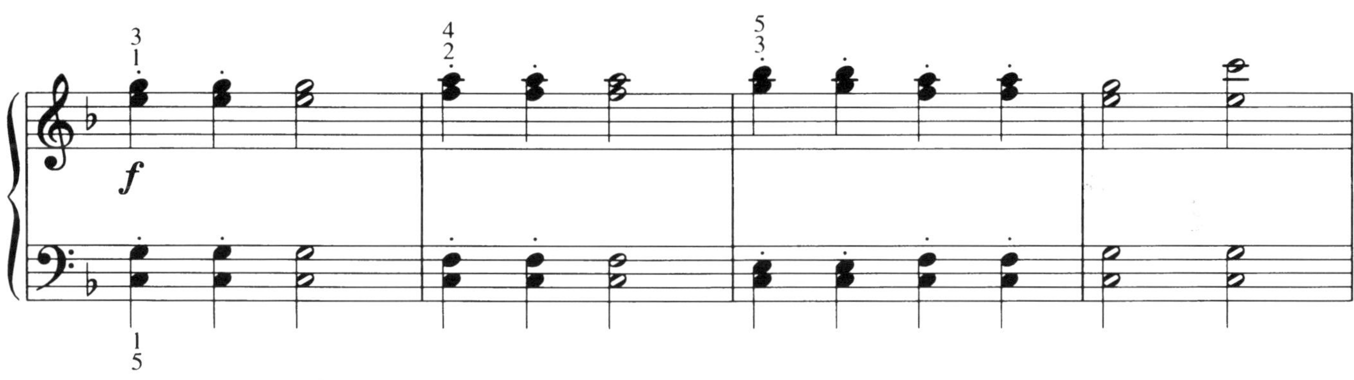

D.C. al Fine

CONSOLATION

Johann Friedrich Burgmüller

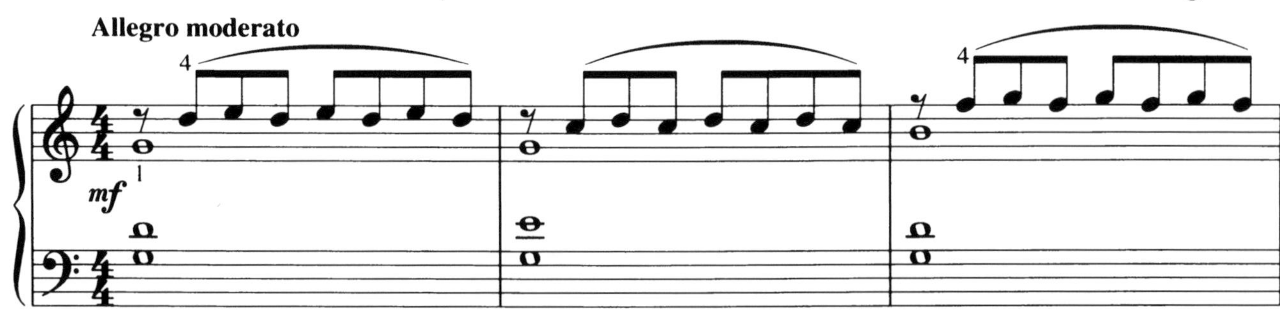

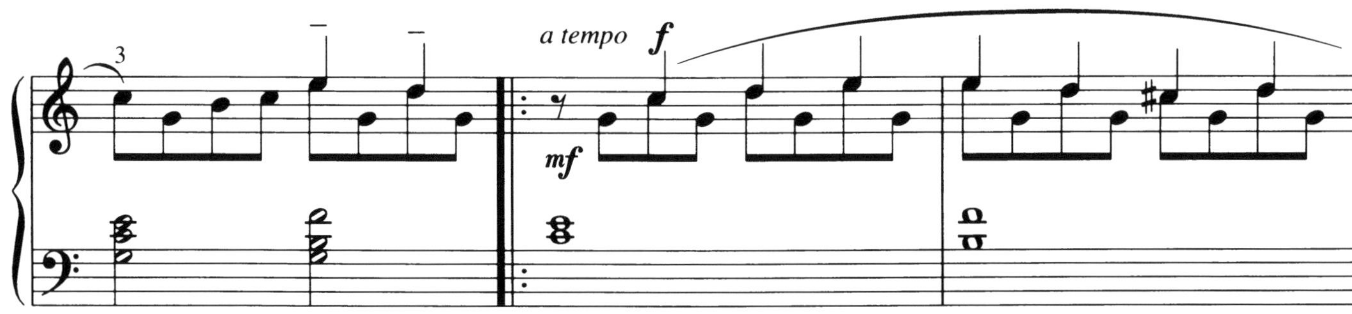

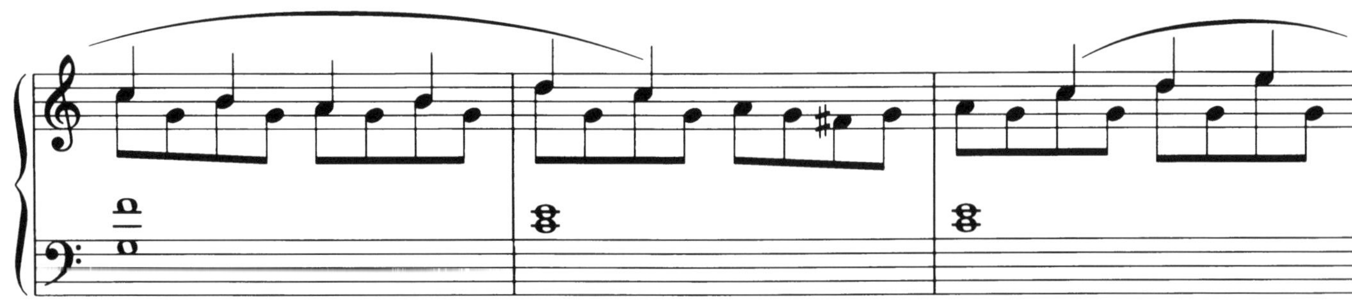

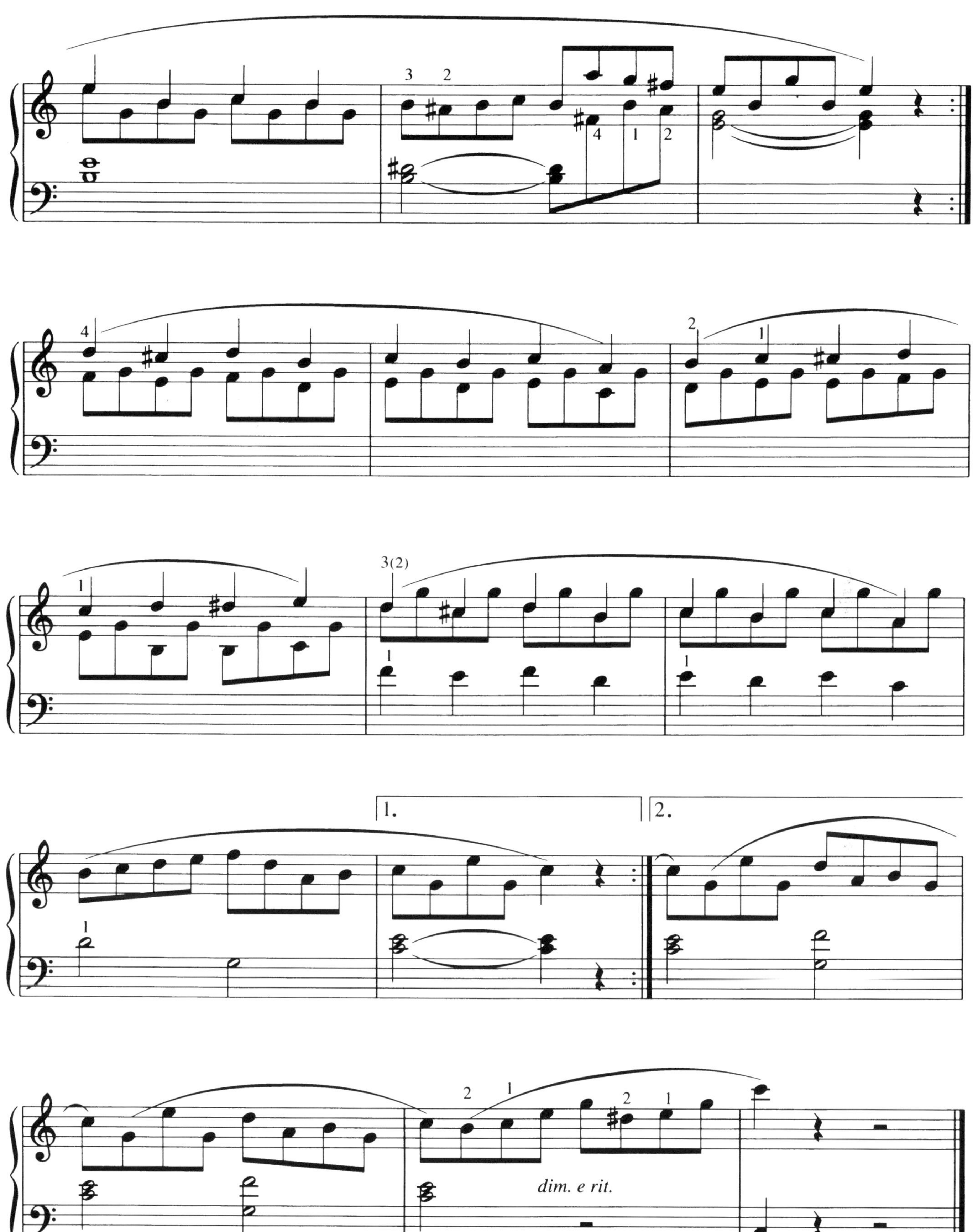
dim. e rit.

JEAN LOUIS GOBBAERTS (1835–1886)
Gobbaerts originally signed his compositions with other names, such as Streabbog (Gobbaerts backwards), Ludovic, and Levy. As well as the method book he wrote, this Belgian composer gave us over 1,200 pieces for the piano.

MELODIE

Jean Louis Gobbaerts

mf
mp
D.C. al Coda
rit.
Coda
f
p

MONODIQUE

Uri Ayn Rovner

PARADE

Uri Ayn Rovner

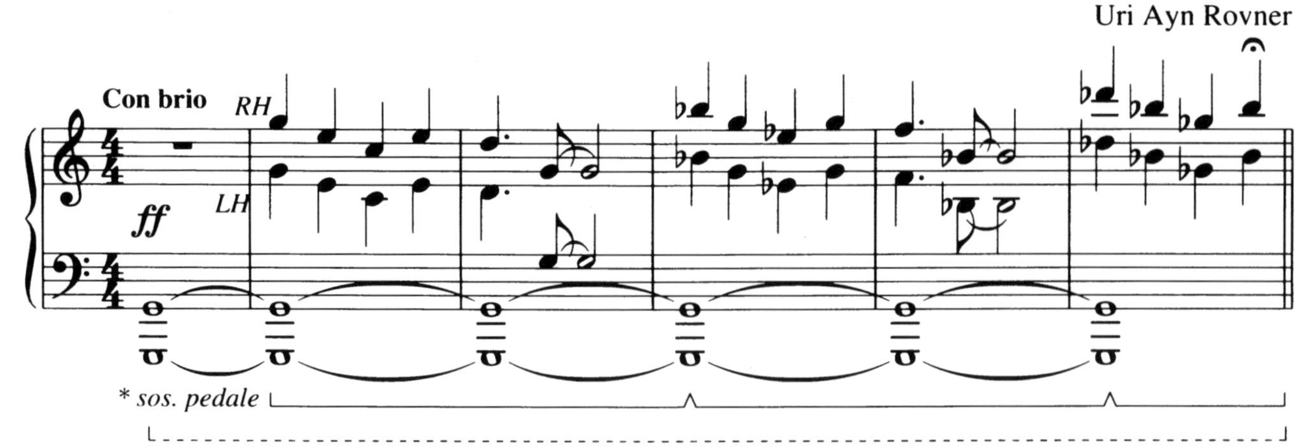

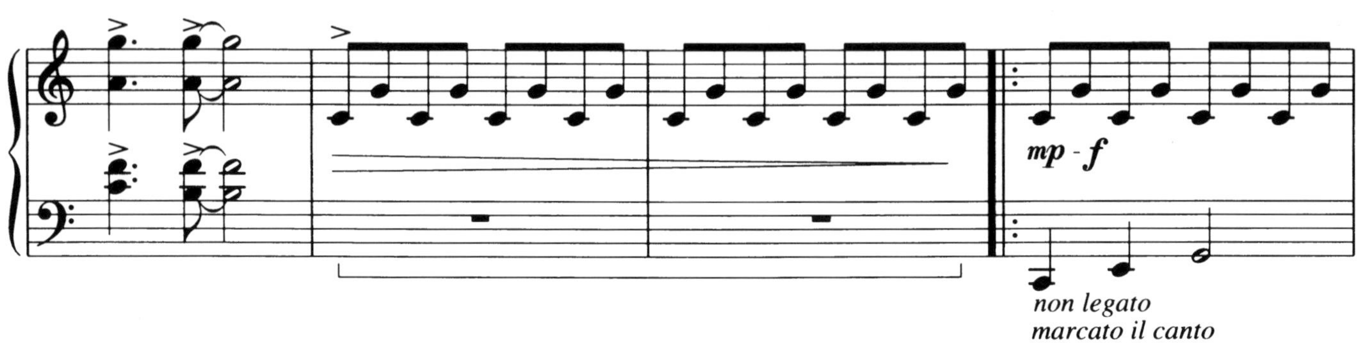

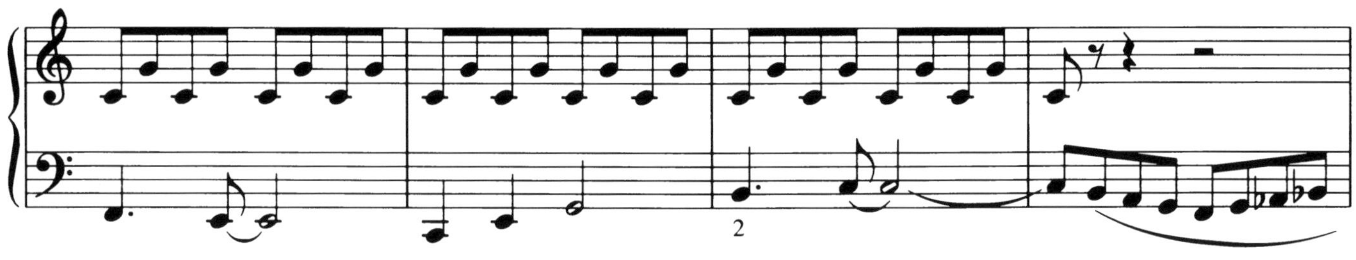

*Damper pedal markings apply if sostenuto pedal is used. If sostenuto pedal is not available,
  damper pedal may remain down for first 6 measures.

2.
ff
cresc.
8va
loco
loco
8va
LH
2/4
4/4
4/4
poco a poco rit. e dim.
5/2
mp
a tempo
ff
23

SONG WITHOUT WORDS

Stephen Heller

Made in the USA
Monee, IL
08 July 2026